Louise

Casey

D0435299

Elliot

Diego

Charles & Bethany

Maxine

Amelia

Mr. Hernandez

Lucy

What are we even doing with our lives?

words by Chelsea Marshall, pictures by Mary Dauterman

DEY ST.
An Imprint of WILLIAM MORROW

Welcome to Digi Valley! The residents of Digi Valley are busy people with busy, modern lives.

organic carrots

Most workers work indoors, but some workers work outdoors. Some who work indoors will take their lunch outdoors just to take pictures and show the world how #blessed they are.

roof garden

start-up
office

retail store

latte

aggressive
canvasser

strawberry
phone

only 1

Some work from home, some work for themselves. Some don't work at all, even though they may tweet constantly about their #hecticsched.

What does *your* daddy even do?
What does *your* mommy even do?
What do *you* even do?
Do you even have a *job*?

Here in Digi Valley lots of people come to the Busy Bean for caffeine and free wi-fi. The slow-drip, cruelty-free, pesticide-free coffee is double the cost of a meal so people cruise the internet for hours to get their money's worth. The internet lets us connect with other people around the world. So, while everybody's in the same room together, they are all talking to people they can't even see. LIKE MAGIC.

arabica beans

wi-fi

TIP, BUTTHO

bran muffins

The barista, Bella, works hard for her tips so she can get extra cash to pay off her student loans. She went to school for photography and while her Instagram has 750k followers, she hasn't been able to monetize it yet.

Everyone in the coffee shop is doing something different but they are all very, very busy.

ELECT
DIANNA
FLURMPH

BerryBook

Sadie and Frances are editing their web series, *Les Filles Petant*, which is all about their lives as twentysomethings farting around.

Freelancer Frank is here today to complete his design gig for the local urban farm. Farmer Natasha has asked Frank to redesign her website, and he's putting in the final touches.

americano

Not many people have laundry in their apartments in this town, so they have to go to a special place to do it.

FREE ((WIFI))

earbuds

Environmental lawyer Erin listens to a podcast while she does her family's laundry. She usually uses an all-natural detergent but secretly "cheats" and uses bleach from time to time.

ANNA FLURMPH

HAT MORE DO YOU ANT FROM ME?

political poster

Annie is an illustrator who likes to stream her favorite web series while her undies dry.

noise-canceling headphones

air conditioner

scaffolding

ACME 321-1141 CONSTRUCTION

Most people in Digi Valley live in little apartments in large buildings. Everyone is close in proximity but somehow they all live in their own worlds.

Some neighbors are strange, some are loud. And some you don't even know are there, except when they are fighting or doing it. That's when the quiet neighbors become really, really loud.

Realtor Rick is going to show an apartment for rent!
Looks like there will be some new tenants soon.
What kind of neighbors will they be?

Digi Valley is a popular place to live and finding a home is very stressful.

salesmanship

Steven, the house mouse

claw-foot tub

Realtor Rick is trying to rent teeny-tiny apartments with weird smells. He loves a good challenge. This apartment costs $4K per month, and Rick promises these two lovebirds a lifetime of intimacy with a bathtub for a bed.

Bethany, a beauty blogger, and Charles, a new media consultant at the hot new ride-share company Ryde Nice, take it after doing quick finance calculations on their phones.

After all, who wouldn't want to stand on the toilet to microwave a burrito while your boyfriend clips his toenails two feet away? #relationshipgoals

tall box

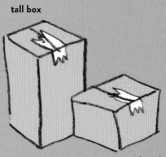

short box

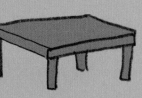

family
heirloom

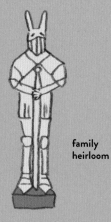

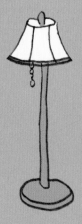

queen-size mattress

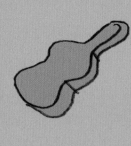

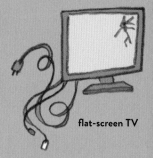

flat-screen TV

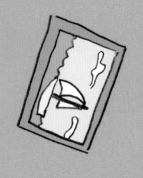

miscellaneous boxes

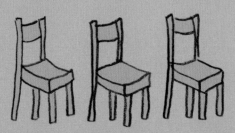

The apartment next
door to the one Rick
is showing is relatively
big but rent is high, so
the tenants rent out
their spare room to
travelers from around
the world.

Frances and Sadie use
the extra money to
fund their web series
while their parents
back in Indiana pay
the rest of the rent.

succulent

suspicious
fedora

Their tenant tonight is a peculiar one. He has not spoken a word and seems to have only packed a case of salami.

salami?

Frances and Sadie's window can see directly into their neighbors' apartment across the way.

They all know what one another looks like dancing in the nude and know their most embarrassing TV shows, but would never dare to make eye contact on the street.

Cat Landlord

tea

Dan and Cheryl live with their youngest son, Luke.

The only time this family comes together without angst is to watch *Cat Landlord*, the most popular reality show on TV. Luke's mom doesn't hesitate to point out that even the cat has a job.

neighbors

decaf coffee

loafers

Luke is thirty-one. Yes, he has a graduate degree, but for the MILLIONTH time, he does not know what he's doing with his life. Stop asking.

This is the next house to be featured on the reality show *Cat Landlord*. It has to be top of the line, so it's big enough to meet building codes but not so big that it holds back the #drama.

trying to look busy

hard hat

workplace disaster

Since *Cat Landlord* started eight years ago, people can't get enough. It's about a real estate mogul cat who has new, crazy tenants every season.

Last season, there was an out-of-control snake family overcoming their lisps.

This season's new tenants are the Hoppers, a family of eleven. Cat Landlord is building them a house large enough for all their personalities, but construction is behind schedule.

Luckily, Frances and Sadie's salami renter packed up early and the Hoppers can stay the night.

hot plate

candy

All of this mess is making the disgruntled Hoppers wonder how far they're willing to go to make it in show business.

accident

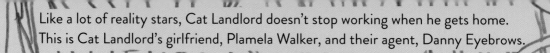
Like a lot of reality stars, Cat Landlord doesn't stop working when he gets home.
This is Cat Landlord's girlfriend, Plamela Walker, and their agent, Danny Eyebrows.

Only 1 U social

boom mic

agent

Danny Eyebrows represents all the Big Cat Talent, but not-so-secretly wants to be a star himself.

A star on her own show, *Wut's with the Walkers?*, Plam is known for her curvaceous tail, but don't let that fool you: she's a business lady through and through. You try getting millions of people to watch you and your family do nothing at all for over a decade.

Turns out, there's a lot that goes into creating reality. The camerarabbit, soundduck, and especially the producers have to make sure the reality is interesting enough for the masses. While the crew works around her, Plam sends off a selfie for her millions of fans on Only 1 U to see. Multitasking is a very valuable skill in this town.

A common issue Plamela and any internet-using person experiences is the troll. Since she's famous, she gets attacked by tons of trolls who love to message her stupidly offensive things. All day, every day.

❤ 41,679

Plamela stay hydrated, fill urself with adventure, water n life <3

Trollo ACTUALLY, U SHOULD WAKE UP #CHEMTRAILS

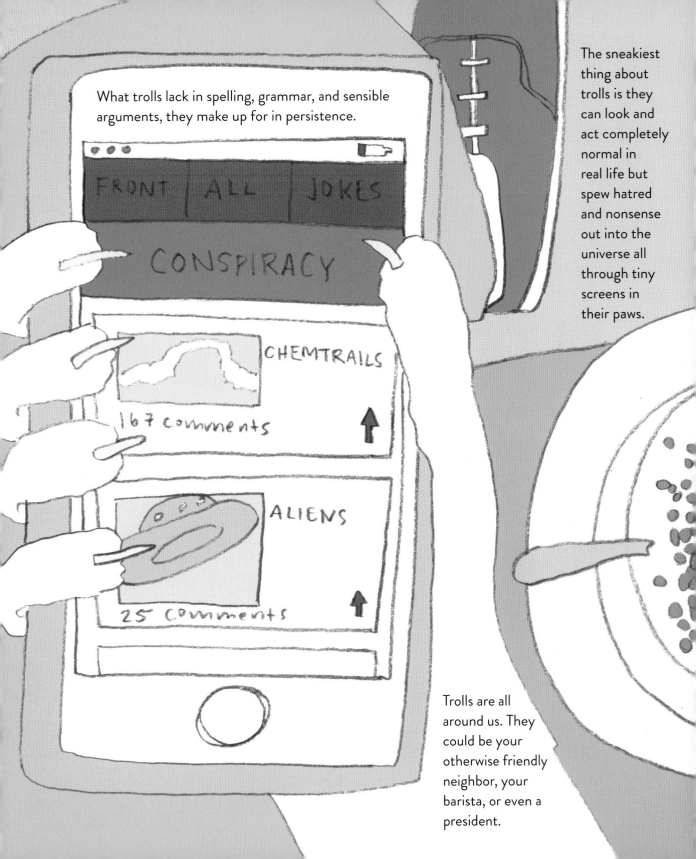

What trolls lack in spelling, grammar, and sensible arguments, they make up for in persistence.

FRONT | ALL | JOKES

CONSPIRACY

CHEMTRAILS

167 comments

ALIENS

25 comments

The sneakiest thing about trolls is they can look and act completely normal in real life but spew hatred and nonsense out into the universe all through tiny screens in their paws.

Trolls are all around us. They could be your otherwise friendly neighbor, your barista, or even a president.

Welcome to Only 1 U, a start-up social platform that all the celebs love. The app is simple and addicting: when users upload a selfie, they get points. If the selfie has bad lighting or angles, or is taken in a bathroom mirror, the user loses points. This social currency is ultimately meaningless but people eat it up.

hoverboard

succulent

This is a Very Fun place to work, complete with hoverboards, nap pods, Hacky Sack rooms, and on-site therapy. The average age of the employees is twenty-three and once you hit thirty, you're basically dead.

All of them are LOLing and HAHAing but you'd never know it because it's all being communicated over the ~cloud~.

Lots of people make up the company: accountants, selfie-content creators pushing the boundaries of self-expression, the dude who somehow keeps getting promoted but no one knows what he does, and, of course, the brave comment moderators.

The comment moderators have the exhausting task of wrangling the trolls and making them behave.

very amused

selfie

YAY

PLAM

TROLL DETECTED

This is the ~cloud~ where everyone's secrets are stored. No one knows how it works or where exactly it's located but they upload everything to it anyway.

download

friend

jokes

bot

doc

foodstagram

internet search hole

password

lol wut

headphones

folders

trash

cold brew

to-do list

☐ go outside
☐ be present
☐ call mom
☑ eat lunch

vitamins

MULTI GUMMI

burrito

window washer

@LeotheFreshest

@MuppMirandy

everything bagel

@MuppMirandy and @LeotheFreshest, both fifteen years old, are here to tell the team what's hot and, most important, what's not.

@LeotheFreshest is getting paid $10K and Miranda is getting paid $7K for an hour of their time. Yes, they do the same job but she gets paid less. You're right, it doesn't make sense.

In this modern age, people love to go from meeting to meeting with the illusion of importance but few people actually know what they're doing.

teleconference

At this meeting, CEO Shawna is bringing together her marketing team with some of the top teen influencers on the internet. What teens want is always changing and companies love to desperately chase it.

CEO coach

WHAT DO TEENS LIKE?

INSIGHTS

invisible speakers

The lobby is a very important part of conveying the vibe of a company. Music and decor need to be perfect.

Maxine is the receptionist. She makes sure all the people and all the food get to where they're going on time.

lunch delivery

1 million followers and counting

online orders

only 1 u

No one in this town has doormen or proper mailboxes at home so they all have to get their mail sent to work. While Maxine sorts the mail, she's thinking about her own start-up, Max Relax, an app that makes relaxation as efficient as possible. It's really stressing her out.

At Only 1 U, there is a texture wall for guests to touch while they wait, meant to evoke various feelings or memories like calmness, childhood, focus, and beast mode.

Luke

empty briefcase

Luke is here interviewing for a web designer position. His mom made him wear a full suit, and, looking around, Luke realizes this was a huge mistake. He's touching the calm texture. Sitting next to him is freelancer Frank, who's not so sure he wants to stay freelance but also is not so sure he wants a 10(ish) to 6(ish) job.

There are all sorts of fun products to see and tasty treats to try at the farmers market.

farm-to-table flowers

eggs

MAYO NOICE!

vinegar

honey

BEEZY TOWN

Over here is the artisanal beekeeper who sings to his bees.

A new mayonnaise stand called Mayo NOICE just opened up. They serve "deconstructed mayo": a hard-boiled egg and some vinegar for a cool twelve bucks.

After his interview, Frank walks over to the farmers market nearby to catch up with his client Natasha, the rooftop farmer. Today, her four-year-old, Shade, came with her to the market.

He's supposed to be helping but he's cramming for his next test.

Everyone comes here to take a rest from looking at their phones (but not for TOO long: you gotta post that selfie from the market online ASAP, #soquaint).

Natasha is an urban farmer, which means everything she sells at the farmers market is grown right here on her roof.

Her wife is an environmental lawyer who travels a lot defending the environment. They are expecting their second child in a few months. Their son, Shade, is as precocious as it gets and "would rawther die" (his words) than get a new sibling.

Today, Natasha has some visitors: her son's class is here to learn about farming, and while they're at it, a new language. They're pointing to each vegetable and translating it to HTML.

If you can't multitask, how are you even functioning anymore?

organic dirt

baby in there!

heirloom tomatoes

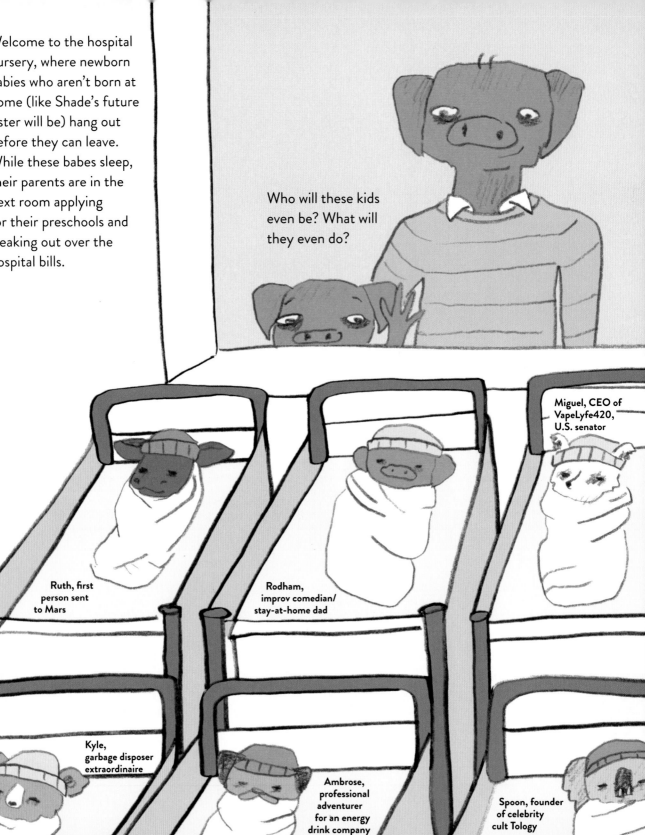

Welcome to the hospital nursery, where newborn babies who aren't born at home (like Shade's future sister will be) hang out before they can leave. While these babes sleep, their parents are in the next room applying for their preschools and freaking out over the hospital bills.

Who will these kids even be? What will they even do?

Miguel, CEO of VapeLyfe420, U.S. senator

Ruth, first person sent to Mars

Rodham, improv comedian/ stay-at-home dad

Kyle, garbage disposer extraordinaire

Ambrose, professional adventurer for an energy drink company

Spoon, founder of celebrity cult Tology

the world

acoustic guitar

safety helmet

This is the very advanced preschool Infinity Circle. All of the students' parents applied to this school years before their children were even conceived. And now they're here, prepping for college so they can get the right job, make enough money, and buy themselves a burial plot that will turn them into a tree in the best park.

It's so crazy raising kids these days! With so many options for parenting, everyone secretly thinks they're doing it wrong. Except Janet and Shaka, who love giving unsolicited advice. Everyone hates them.

The playground is a place where kids can be kids. They learn different social dynamics through play, in a safe environment heavily monitored to make sure they're doing it "right." Sometimes it seems like kids know how to deal with each other better than any adult.

helmet

up slide

down slide

Amelia likes to throw around a robotic ball that records her strength progress. One day, this information will be sent to colleges to fortify her chances of getting a softball scholarship.

Cindy is on her sixth day of trying to lick her elbow.

Hector over here likes to act out his one-person show during recess, no matter his audience size.

scooter

CAUTION

PLAY AT YOUR OWN RISK

phone

Miranda prefers to retreat into her phone when she gets anxious.

Here's seven-year-old Miranda's phone.
She isn't makin' friends but she IS makin' $$$.

There are many ways to get around Digi Valley, from cars to buses to scooters. But the most popular and most reliable is the subway, called Digi Vroom.

This line is the Red Line and it gets people from one side of town to another in twenty minutes, give or take . . . a lot.

Great days, bad days, stinky days, sexy days. They all happen on the train.

sadness

Today, teacher Alexis Hernandez is rushing to catch the train back home but just missed it. She's had a tough day already, getting yelled at by parents who can't believe she gave their children a "B" on a math test. The conductor closing the door in her face is just enough to get those tears flowing. While it doesn't seem like it, Ms. Hernandez's day just got very exciting: crying in public is a rite of passage for people here in Digi Valley. Now she's an official resident.

podcast

teen

mysterious stink?

In case anyone was worried this moment wasn't documented: Tara the teen captured it on live video. Teens in this town are the scariest creatures of all. They come at you with insults, and any adults who defend themselves are rendered even lamer. It's a lose-lose for everyone. Except the teens.

public radio

Zuki is one of the people having a horrible day on the train. He spilled his bag and now everything is on display.

Perhaps the most exhilarating part of the ride is showtime, when two men do acrobatic tricks, usually during rush hour. Everyone is always amazed at their abilities while being terrified of getting kicked in the face.

It's impressive how much can get packed in a small space. But a word to the wise: never, ever get in an empty train car lest you care to smell a dirty sock filled with poop that's been lying in the sun for hours. This man made that mistake before switching over to this jam-packed car. He may never be the same.

showtime

nail clipper

queasiness

As efficient as the train is, sometimes it stops for "a sick passenger," which could mean anything. It doesn't help that today there's a momentary blackout and no one can understand the announcers.

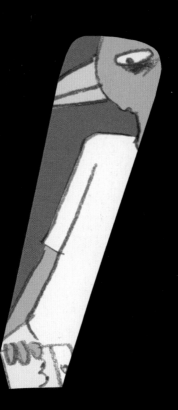

In other towns, people would get worried.
But here, they just get annoyed.

bus

camper van

scooter

used sedan

subway

motorcycle

pickup

taxi

bicycle

skateboard

golf cart

There's a jukebox in the corner but it's really just a streaming device meant to look like a record player. Unfortunately, Diego put three hours of his band's electronica music on it, and there seems to be no end in sight.

gender-neutral bathroom

beer

dinero

Datrr

Diego is the bartender here. He knows everyone's secrets but he couldn't care less. He's a bartender at night, an IT guy during the day, and a ride-share driver in his spare time. Student loans are overwhelming and it's tough to stay on top of them, even with three jobs.

Frank and Bella are sitting at the bar, swiping through potential matches on their phones. They'd probably be a perfect match but are too busy looking down to find each other.

This is baby-friendly Brewski's, one of the most popular bars in Digi Valley.

A lot happens in a bar. People go on first dates, look for people to bone, meet up with friends, and have too-boozy happy hours with their coworkers.

shots

pinot grigio

cosmo

dad

son

stroller

Instead of finding a date in the bar, they can find one in the palms of their paws.

tru luv

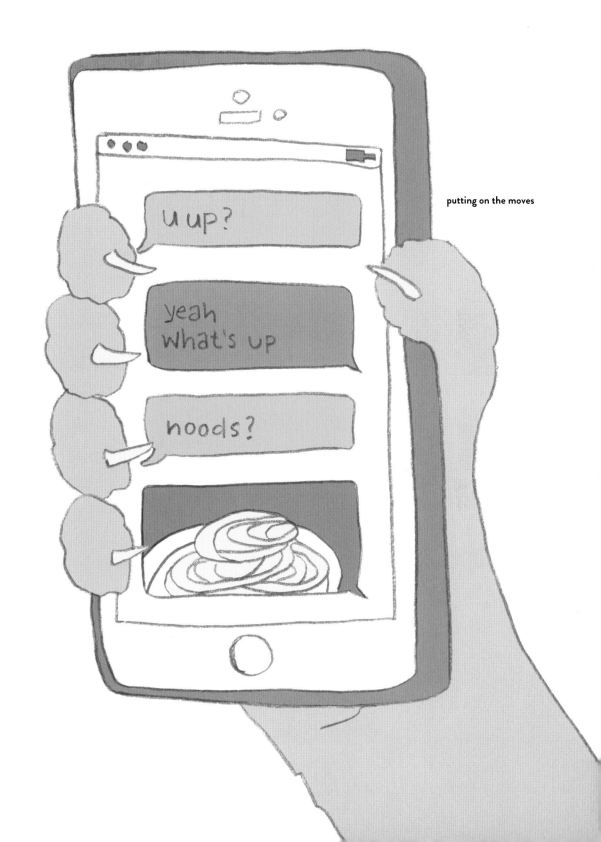

Sometimes after a late-night date, there is a very awkward morning after.

Darren is in town for a conference and rented Sadie and Frances' spare room for the night. He clearly was not expecting company but he was wooed by Lauren's sense of humor and a few too many tequila shots.

sneakers

duffel bag

fast food

Darren's phone

Neither remembers the other's name but both know they
need to get out of there and quick. Thank god for brunch.

Lauren's phone

EGG YOU

Brunch is a sacred time here, just like church, but drunker and more 'grammable.

Over here, Amy and Tina are catching up after a month of canceling and rescheduling on each other. It's amazing either of them made it at all and their excitement is highlighted with deafening squeals of delight.

MENU

Bottomless Brunch

carafe

Waiter Wynd has to give himself pep talks before going out onto the restaurant floor.

RSELF

One of the hottest places is Egg Yourself, a spot where people groggy from the night before wait three hours to get in. Friends come together after drinking all night, only to continue the festivities alongside eggs, pancakes, and cheap alcohol.

espresso machine

server

pancakes

food-stagram

It is no easy feat being in the service industry, but working hungover among loud, drunk people is next-level bad. He should follow the lead of his coworker Casey and just drink with the patrons. Whoever invented unlimited mimosa brunches is both a genius and a monster.

free-range bacon

bottomless
mimosa

latte

gluten-free
waffles

avocado
toast

Bloody
Mary

soy latte

eggs
Benedict

The only place more hectic than a brunch-time restaurant is the kitchen making the food. Especially at a place as popular as Egg Yourself.

Ever since reality star Plamela came in and uploaded a pic of the PB+J cocktail, the restaurant has been packed.

lettuce

butter

avocado toast

waffles

Chef Amanda is a true artist with her food and her soul dies just a little bit every time someone only orders avocado toast.

over-easy egg

A table sent a dish back, claiming there was too much gluten in the pancakes. It takes a lot for chef Amanda not to go out there and start screaming.

A trip to the park to vape a medicinal herb always helps her take the edge off.

kid leashes

This is one of the most vibrant parts of the city, where people can escape from everyday technologies.

Over here is the "selfie tree," known for having the best light.

lunch

rescue dog

purebred dog

aggressive
canvasser

camera

tourists

Much to the chagrin
of the park purists,
there was recently
a camera set up
for an indoor
cycling class
down the street.

That way, the people
riding stationary bikes
a few blocks down can
feel like they're outside
without actually
going there.

Soon enough,
the whole place
will have free wi-fi.

A lot of workers in Digi Valley come to the
park for breaks. Chefs, nurses, teachers,
CEOs—they all come here to decompress,
eat lunch, and, unfortunately, vape.

Digi Valley has some of the best doctors in the world, but because health care is so expensive, it can be a real pain to get the care you need.

Lucy's child sneezed and now she's afraid he's dying (he's not), and poor Pedro is getting "text neck" from using his phone too much. All the office phones are ringing but the receptionists can't be bothered to answer them.

mom

Some people don't mind the doctor, some people hate the doctor, and some think they always need to go. Whatever it is, Dr. Simons is here for her patients (unless she doesn't carry their insurance).

Dr. Simons is exasperated after three appointments in a row pleading with parents to just vaccinate their damn kids.

cotton balls

skeleton

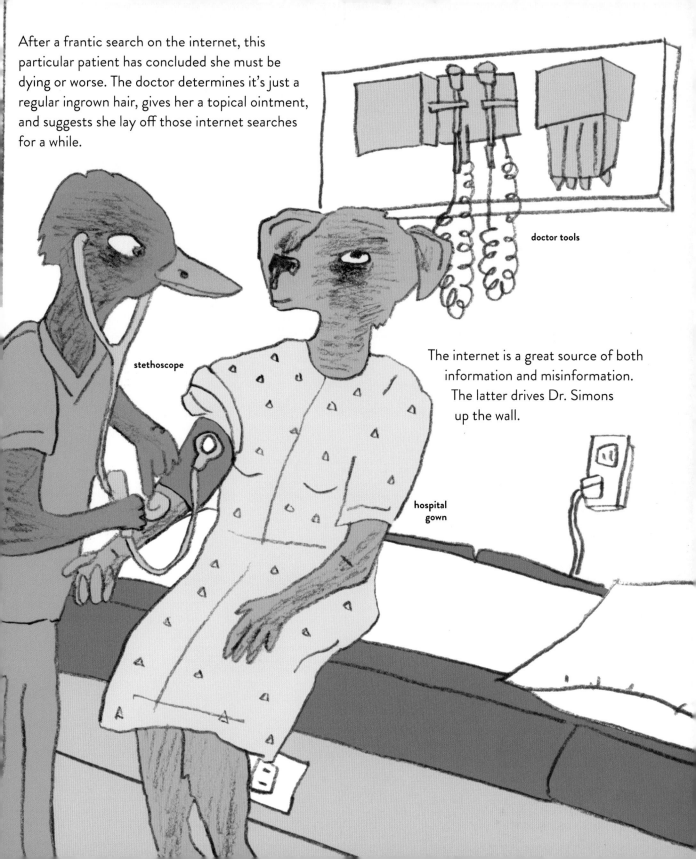

After a frantic search on the internet, this particular patient has concluded she must be dying or worse. The doctor determines it's just a regular ingrown hair, gives her a topical ointment, and suggests she lay off those internet searches for a while.

doctor tools

The internet is a great source of both information and misinformation. The latter drives Dr. Simons up the wall.

stethoscope

hospital gown

indoor palm

Just like there are doctors for the body, equally important are the doctors for the mind.

People love to walk around and post about their perfect lives, but people inner lives can often tell a different story.

WOW...

notepad

corduroy

Today, Cat Landlord and Plamela, the famous "perfect couple," are in couples therapy. They each think the other spends too much time online but neither is willing to scale it back. At this point in the session, neither party is speaking to the other and the therapist is longing for a stiff drink.

Plam's phone

Cat Landlord's phone

The people of Digi Valley have come to expect everything immediately, from food delivery to medicine to transportation. That's where Ryde Nice comes in: it's THE service that allows you to call for a car at any time of day at the click of a button.

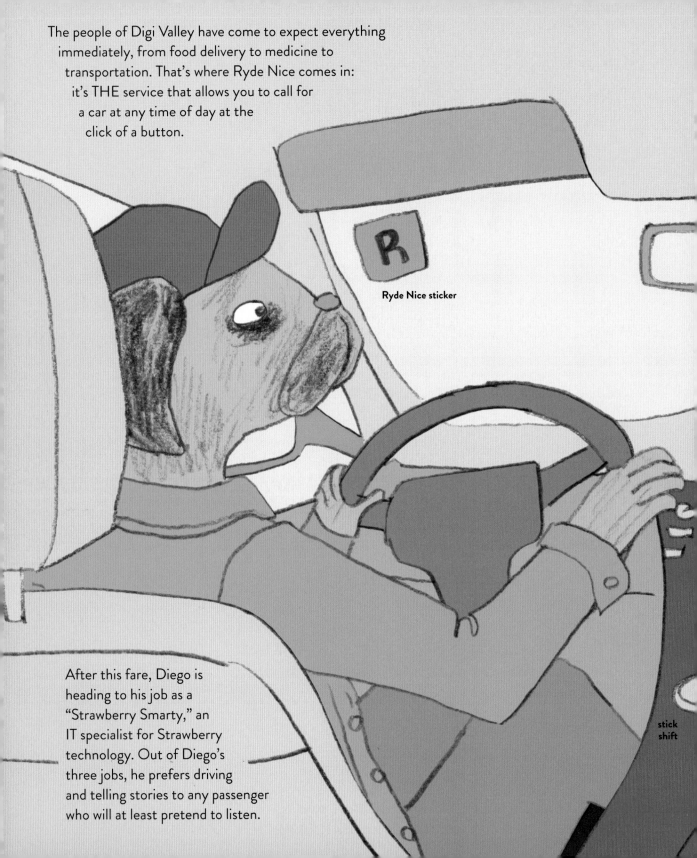

Ryde Nice sticker

stick shift

After this fare, Diego is heading to his job as a "Strawberry Smarty," an IT specialist for Strawberry technology. Out of Diego's three jobs, he prefers driving and telling stories to any passenger who will at least pretend to listen.

Too flustered by all the trash in the backseat and subsequently having to sit in the front, Plamela has just realized she got in the wrong car. But she's feeling adventurous and wants to see where this one goes.

rearview mirror

This particular car smells like a mix of a urinal cake and old froyo. Diego will let you play whatever music you want as long as he can use his DJ scratching app over the tunes.

low rating

EGO'S
IXXX

Today, the Strawberry company just released the newest gadget: contact lenses that allow you to record the world around you and share it directly to social media. It's called StrawMe and it's very controversial.

There was a different, buggy version a few months ago that uploaded users' videos to the internet without permission.

Strawberry
Smarty

Things got too sexy and too awkward in Digi Valley and no one likes to talk about it.

Nevertheless, the store is packed with people who just love to be the first ones to get the newest commodity, no matter how frivolous. Stop judging! We all create meaning in different ways and this is theirs.

checkout
bear

PAM

BRAN

seltzer

tortilla chips

different
seltzer

In the midst of the tech boom
and organic farming trends, Urthy D'lite
is a favorite among the Digi Valley residents.
This location sometimes goes so far as to have a
local band play, in order to keep people coming back.

There has been an increase in grocery-cart-related
injuries since the age of smartphones; while many
people come for the cereal, they leave with a lawsuit.

Here in Digi Valley, people choose to eat some animals and not others.
It's all pretty arbitrary and no one likes to think about it.

What keeps people coming back is the sandwiches: Urthy D'lite has the
best in town. Luigi is the butcher and all his sandwich recipes are credited
to his grandmother. He will never tell anyone that his
name is actually Ron and all of his recipes can be found
on the side of a hamburger-mix box.

meat

meat

meat

18.99

8.99

99

6.99

meat

This candidate, Dianna Flurmph, hasn't been in a grocery store herself in years but she's trying to be "relatable." There are a lot of hoops she has to jump through as a candidate: she has to be approachable but strong, smart but not TOO smart. Despite her efforts, they'll continue to hate her. It's exhausting.

Urthy D'lite

hybrid sedan

sandwich

Hank the wi-fi repairotter loves being late for appointments but this time he'll be extra late.
This traffic jam means Digi Valley residents are going to have to wait for their
free wi-fi a bit longer. But at least Hank got his sandwich.

During jams, everyone loves to honk because they are SO BOOORED.
Pro tip: it becomes more bearable if you think of it as them just saying hello!

curb

sandwich

very wifi

Hank finally makes it to the park to install the controversial wi-fi, breaking through the rows of protesters and tourists. He has to install it down in the ground so as not to mess up the precious selfie tree. He tinkers, he plots, and just as he is almost done, he gets a text message.

roof garden

no wi-fi

no wi-fi

no wi-fi

ve
wif

Laws of impulsivity will him to check it and he accidentally drops his tools down the hole. *Clink, clank, clunk, BAM!*

Oh no! Something has gone horribly wrong!

Hank shut off the electricity and with it, the wi-fi for the WHOLE TOWN.

Everything is silent for a second. This town has never been without connection to the outside world . . .

Chelsea Marshall and Mary Dauterman
are lady friends with lady animals.

HarperCollins books may be purchased for educational, business, or sales promotional use. For information, please e-mail the Special Markets Department at SPsales@harpercollins.com.

FIRST EDITION

Library of Congress Cataloging-in-Publication Data has been applied for.

ISBN 978-0-06-265418-2

17 18 19 20 21   QG   10 9 8 7 6 5 4 3 2 1

Cat Landlord

Olivia

Benjamin

VOTE 4 ME
DIANNA
FLURMPH

Dianna Flurmph

Frank

The Out-of-Towner

Hank

Bella

MILK

Zuki & Little Zuki